ULTIMATE QUESTIONS

JOHN BLANCHARD

D0368444

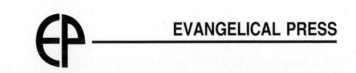

EVANGELICAL PRESS

EVANGELICAL PRESS
Faverdale North, Darlington, Co.Durham, DL3 0PH, England

P.O. Box 825, Webster, NY 14580, USA

© Evangelical Press 1987
First published 1987
This edition 2007.

ISBN 0 85234 534 8
ISBN-13-978 0 85234 534 4
British Library Cataloguing-in-Publication Data available

All Scripture quotations are taken from the New King James Version (NKJV) Copyright © 1982 by Thomas Nelson, Inc.Used by permission. All rights reserved.

This booklet is also published in Afrikaans, Albanian, Burmese, Bulgarian, Chichewa, Chinese (class), Chinese (simp), Croatian, Czech, Dutch, Estonian, Finnish, French, German, Greek, Hungarian, Italian, Japanese, Korean, Latvian, Macedonian, Mongolian, Norwegian, Polish, Portuguese, Romanian, Russian, Serbian, Setswana, Slovak, Slovenian, Spanish, Swahili, Swedish, Tagalog, Thai, Turkish, Ukranian, Vietnamese, Zulu, Xhosa.

Photographs reproduced by permission of the following photographers and agencies:
John Blanchard (Pages 8,13,18,19,21 ,23-25,27,29,30)
Malcolm Boulton (Page 3)
I. Allen Cash Photo Library (Cover, pages 4,6,9,22)
Bob Obbard (Pages 10,11,14,16,20)
Pictorial Press (Page 12)
Rex Features Ltd. (Page 26)
Science Photo Library (Page 5)
Syndication International (Page 15)
Clifford Tanner (Pages 7,17,28)

Layout and design by KNR Graphics
58 Rectory Lane, Long Ditton, Surrey, KT6 5HW
Printed in Singapore, by SNP Security Printing Pte Ltd

Life is full of questions. Some are trivial, some more serious – and some tremendously important.

Even as you read these words, you may have questions about your health, your financial situation, your job, your family or your future.

But the greatest, the ultimate questions, are about God and your relationship to him. Nothing in life is more important than this. Good health, financial stability, secure employment, a contented family and a hopeful future are all things that people want. Yet even these are temporary and eventually pointless unless you have a living relationship with God, one that is clear and certain – and will last for ever.

In the following pages you will discover why such a relationship is so urgently needed – and how it is possible.

The questions that follow are the most serious and important that anyone could ask. The answers are those that everyone needs.

Please read these pages thoroughly and carefully – and if necessary more than once.

You cannot afford to miss their message.

Is anyone there?

This is the fundamental question. If God does not exist, searching for him is pointless: *for he who comes to God must believe that He is.*[1] While it is impossible to 'prove' God in a mathematical sense, the evidence is very convincing.

Take the existence of the universe. To call it the result of an 'accident' raises many questions – and answers none. The same is true of the 'Big Bang' theory. Where, for instance, did the raw materials come from? Not even a 'big bang' can make something out of nothing! The evolutionary idea is widespread, but just as weak; how can 'nothing' evolve into 'something', let alone earth's amazingly complex life forms?[2]

All other theories are equally fragile. The only satisfactory explanation is this: *In the beginning God created the heavens and the earth.* Our world is not the random result of a gigantic fluke involving ingredients that were 'always there'. Instead, *the worlds were framed by the word of God, so that things which are seen were not made of things which are visible.* Creation had a beginning, and it was God who brought it into being. *For He spoke, and it was done; He commanded, and it stood fast.*

This is reinforced by the amazing order and design seen everywhere and by the universal laws which hold everything together, from the vastness of outer space to microscopic organisms. But design demands a designer and laws a law-giver – and God is both! *God, who made the world and everything in it, since He is Lord of heaven and earth.*

But the strongest 'creation evidence' is man himself. Unlike other living creatures, man has something we call 'personality'; he makes intelligent choices, has a conscience and can distinguish between right and wrong. He is capable of love and compassion. Above all, he has an instinct to worship. Where did he get these qualities? Neither evolution nor an avalanche of accidents could have produced them. The clearest answer is this: *And the Lord God formed man of the dust of the ground, and breathed into his nostrils the breath of life; and man became a living being.* Man is not an accident: he is *fearfully and wonderfully made* by the Creator of the universe.

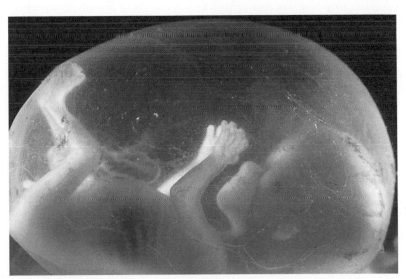

[1] All words in italic type (other than book titles) are quotations from the Bible as indicated on page 32.

[2] This is a major and complex issue, impossible to discuss here. If evolution is a genuine problem to you, read *From Nothing to Nature,* by Prof.E.H.Andrews (Evangelical Press).

Is God speaking?

The question is vital. Left to ourselves we are totally ignorant of God. *Can you search out the deep things of God? Can you find out the limits of the Almighty?* God is beyond our understanding and we need him to reveal himself to us.

Creation is one of the main ways he does so. *The heavens declare the glory of God; and the firmament shows his handiwork.* The sheer size of the universe and its amazing balance, variety and beauty reveal a great deal about the God who made it. In creation God shows his stupendous power, awesome intelligence and brilliant imagination. *For since the creation of the world his invisible attributes are clearly seen, being understood by the things that are made, even his eternal power and Godhead, so that they are without excuse.*

When we communicate with one another we rely heavily on words. God also speaks to men through words – the words of the Bible. Nearly 4,000 times in the Old Testament alone (500 times in the first five books) you will find phrases like 'the Lord spoke', 'the Lord commanded' and 'the Lord said'. This is why it is claimed that Scripture *never came by the will of man, but holy men of God spoke as they were moved by the Holy Spirit.*

In no other literature can we find scores of clear and detailed prophecies made by men claiming to speak from God and later fulfilled to the letter. The odds against this happening by chance are too vast to be taken seriously.

Then there is the Bible's impact on people's lives. No other book has had such a life-changing power. Millions of people, over thousands of years, have proved by personal experience that *The law of the Lord is perfect, converting the soul; The testimony of the Lord is sure, making wise the simple. The statutes of the Lord are right rejoicing the heart; The commandment of the Lord is pure, enlightening the eyes.*

After 2,000 years no expert in any field has ever disproved a single statement in the Bible.[3] The reason is this: *All Scripture is given by inspiration of God.* We should therefore accept it *not as the word of men, but as it is in truth, the word of God.*

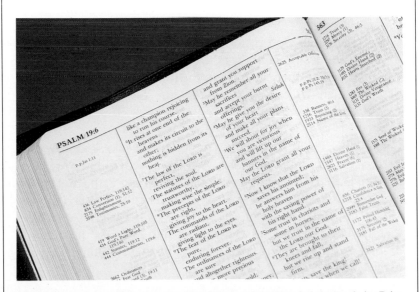

---

[3] If you have serious questions about the Bible read *Nothing but the Truth,* by Brian Edwards (Evangelical Press).

What is God like?

This is obviously the next question to be faced. To acknowledge that God exists is one thing, and to acknowledge him in the general sense that God speaks to us in creation and through the pages of the Bible is another. But we need to know more. What is God actually like?

The Bible gives us many clear and positive answers to this tremendously important question. Here are some of them.

God is personal. God is not a 'thing', power or influence. He thinks, feels, desires and acts in ways that show him to be a living personal Being. But he is not just 'the man upstairs' or some kind of 'superman'. *But the Lord is the true God; he is the living God and the everlasting King.*

God is one. There is only one true God. He says, *I am the first and the last; besides me there is no God.* Yet God has revealed himself as a 'trinity' of three Persons – the Father, the Son (Jesus Christ) and the Holy Spirit, each of whom is truly, fully and equally God. The Bible speaks of the *glory of God the Father;* it says that *the Word* (Jesus Christ) *was God;* and it speaks of *the Spirit of the Lord.* While there is only one God, there are three Persons in the Godhead.

God is Spirit. He has no physical dimensions. He does not have a body, nor does he have any characteristics that can be defined in terms of size and shape. *God is a Spirit, and those who worship him must worship in spirit and truth.* This means that God is invisible. *No one has seen God at any time.* It also means he is not confined to one place at a time, but is everywhere all the time: *'Do I not fill heaven and earth? says the Lord.'* Quite apart from anything else, this means that God is fully aware of everything that happens everywhere. This includes not only everything you do and say, but every thought that passes through your mind.

God is eternal. God has no beginning. In the Bible's words, *from everlasting to everlasting, you are God.* There never was a time when God did not exist and there never will be a time when he will not exist. God describes himself as the one *who is and who was and who is to come.* And he remains eternally the same: *For I am the Lord, I do not change.* All that God ever was he still is and always will be.

God is independent. Every other living being is dependent on people or things, and ultimately on God – but God is totally independent of his creation. He can survive on his own. *Nor is he worshipped with men's hands, as though he needed anything, since he gives to all life, breath, and all things.*

God is holy. *Glorious in holiness, fearful in praises.* There can be no comparison with the holiness of God. *There is none holy like the Lord* who is utterly without fault or defect. The Bible says of him, *You are of purer eyes than to behold evil, and cannot look on wickedness.* And this holy God demands holiness from every one of us. His command to us today is: *Be holy, for I am holy.*

God is just. The Bible says that *the Lord is a God of justice:* and that *righteousness and justice are the foundation of his throne.* God is not only our Creator and Sustainer; he is also our Judge, rewarding and punishing, in time and eternity, with a justice that is perfect and beyond any appeal or dispute.

God is perfect. His knowledge is perfect: *And there is no creature hidden from his sight, but all things are naked and open to the eyes of him to whom we must give account.* God knows everything in the past, present and future, including all our thoughts, words and deeds. His wisdom is perfect and utterly beyond our understanding. *Oh, the depth of the riches both of the wisdom and knowledge of God! How unsearchable are his judgements and his ways past finding out!*

God is sovereign. He is the sole and supreme ruler of the universe, and nothing whatever is outside of his control. *Whatever the Lord pleases he does, in heaven and in the earth.* With God there are no accidents or surprises. He writes all the world's history and *works all things according to the counsel of his will.* God needs no advice or consent for anything he chooses to do. Nor can anyone prevent him doing what he pleases: *No one can restrain his hand or say to him, 'What have you done?'*

God is omnipotent. He is all-powerful. In his own words *Behold I am the Lord, the God of all flesh. Is there anything too hard for me?* This does not mean that God can do anything (he cannot lie, or change, or make mistakes, or sin, or deny himself) but that he can do anything he wishes consistent with his character.

These are just brief sketches of some of the things God has revealed in the Bible about his own nature and character. There are other truths about God in the Bible (and we will look at one of these on page 22) though there are many things about him we cannot possibly understand. He *does great things, and unsearchable, marvellous things without number.* In that sense, *we cannot find him* and no amount of human intelligence or reasoning can change that. This should hardly surprise us. If we could understand God he would be unworthy of our worship.

Who am I?

The pressures and problems of modern living are driving many people to a restless search for meaning and purpose in life. We have seen something of who God is; what about us? Why do we exist? Why are we here? Does human life have any meaning or purpose?

The first thing to get clear is that man does not merely 'exist'. He is more than an accidental accumulation of atoms which all happen to fit together in a convenient package we call 'a human being'. The Bible tells us that he was specifically created by a wise and holy God. *So God created man in his own image; in the image of God he created him; male and female he created them.* Man is more than a highly developed animal or refined ape. He is as different from other creatures as animals are from vegetables and vegetables are from minerals. In terms of size, man is minute compared with the sun, moon and stars, but God has given him a unique and honoured place in the universe.

This is seen in one of God's first commands to man: *have dominion over the fish of the sea, over the birds of the air, and over every living thing that moves on the earth.* Man became God's personal representative on earth, with authority over all other living creatures.

But man was also given special dignity. Being created 'in the image of God' does not mean that he was made the same size and shape of God (we have seen that God does not have 'size' or 'shape'), nor that man was a miniature of God, possessing all his qualities in small quantities. It means that man was created as a spiritual, rational, moral and immortal being, with a nature that was perfect. In other words he was a true reflection of God's holy character.

What is more, man gladly and constantly chose to obey all God's commands and as a result lived in perfect harmony with him. Man had no 'identity crisis' then! He knew exactly who he was and why he was in the world, and he obediently took his God-given place.

But not only was man totally fulfilled and completely satisfied with his position in the world. God was satisfied with man! We know this because the Bible tells us that when his work of creation was complete, with man as its crowning glory, *God saw everything that he had made, and indeed it was very good.* At that point in history, perfect people lived in a perfect environment in a perfect relationship with each other and in perfect harmony with God.

That is hardly the situation today! What happened?

What went wrong?

The straightforward answer to the question is this: *through one man sin entered the world, and death through sin.*

The first man and woman (Adam and Eve) were given great freedom, but also one serious warning: *But from the tree of the knowledge of good and evil you shall not eat, for in the day that you eat the fruit of it, you shall surely die.* This was an ideal test of man's willingness to obey what God said simply because God said it. But the devil tempted Eve to disbelieve and disobey God's words, and she did. *So when the woman saw that the tree was good for food, that it was pleasant to the eyes, and a tree desirable to make one wise, she took of its fruit and ate. She also gave to her husband with her, and he ate.*

At that moment 'sin entered the world'. By his deliberate disobedience man cut himself off from God. Instead of loving God, Adam and Eve were terrified of him: *Adam and his wife hid themselves from the presence of the Lord God among the trees of the garden.* Instead of being assured, confident and happy, their sin had made them ashamed, guilty and afraid.

But God had said that man would die if he disobeyed, and he did. Death means separation from God, and in one terrible moment man became separated from God; he died spiritually. He also began to die physically, and now had a dead soul and a dying body. But that was not all: the children of Adam and Eve inherited their corrupt nature and sinful character. From then on, like pollution at the source of a river, the poison of sin has flowed to all Adam's descendants, *and thus death spread to all men, because all sinned.*

Notice that important word 'all', which obviously includes the writer and the reader of this page. We may never meet on this earth, but we have this in common – we are sinners and we are dying. *If we say we have no sin, we deceive ourselves, and the truth is not in us;* and if we claim not to be dying we are being ridiculous. Fooling around with the facts does nothing to change them.

Many of today's newspaper, television and radio headlines remind us of the fact that the world is in a mess. It is easy to condemn violence, injustice, disorder and wrongdoing in society, but before criticising others ask yourself whether you are perfect and living a life pleasing to a holy God. Are you absolutely honest, pure, loving and selfless? God knows the answers to these questions – and so do you! *For all have sinned and fall short of the glory of God.* You are a sinner by birth, by nature, by practice and by choice, and you urgently need to face the facts – and the consequences.

Is sin serious?

When disease is first diagnosed, it is important to ask the question: 'Is it serious?' It is even more important to ask that question about the spiritual disease of sin. Many people will almost cheerfully admit to being sinners, because they have no idea what this means. They treat it as being 'just human nature', or they shelter behind the fact that 'everybody does it'. But those statements dodge the real issue: is sin serious? Here are some of the things the Bible says about you as a sinner.

You are debased. This does not mean that you are as bad as you can possibly be, nor that you are constantly committing every sin. Nor does it mean that you cannot tell right from wrong, or do things that are pleasant and helpful. But it does mean that sin has invaded every part of your nature and personality – your mind, will, affections, conscience, disposition and imagination. *The heart is deceitful above all things, and desperately wicked.* The root of your trouble is not what you do but what you are! You sin because you are a sinner.

You are defiled. The Bible pulls no punches here: *For from within,* *out of the heart of men, proceed evil thoughts, adulteries, fornications, murders, thefts, covetousness, wickedness, deceit, licentiousness, an evil eye, blasphemy, pride, foolishness.* Notice that the list includes thoughts, words and actions. This shows that in God's sight all sin is equally serious. Some people limit their idea of sin to things like murder, adultery and robbery, but the Bible makes it clear that we have no right to think of sin in this way. Sin is anything that fails to meet God's perfect standards. Anything we say, think or do that is less than perfect is sin. Now face up to this question: *Who can say, I have made my heart clean, I am pure from my sin?* Can you? If not, you are defiled.

You are defiant. The Bible teaches that *sin is lawlessness*: deliberate rebellion against God's authority and law. No civil law forces you to lie, cheat, have impure thoughts or sin in any other way. You choose to sin. You choose to break God's holy law. You deliberately disobey him and that is serious, because *God is a just judge, and God is angry with the wicked every day.* God can never be 'soft' about sin, and you can be sure that not even one sin will go unpunished.

Some small part of God's punishment comes in this life (though we may not recognise it). But the final punishment will be inflicted after death, when on the Day of Judgement *each of us shall give account of himself to God.*

Where do I go from here?

There are many ideas about what happens when we die. Some say we are all annihilated, some say that we all go to heaven. Others believe in a place where sinful souls are prepared for heaven. But nothing in the Bible supports any of these ideas.

Instead, we read this: *it is appointed for men to die once, but after this the judgement.* Those in a right relationship with God will then be welcomed into heaven, to spend eternity in his glorious presence. All others will be *punished with everlasting destruction from the presence of the Lord and from the glory of his power.* The Bible's most common word for this is 'hell'. Here are four important truths about it:

Hell is factual. It is not something 'invented by the church'. The Bible says more about hell than it does about heaven and leaves no doubt about its reality. It speaks of *the condemnation of hell* and of those who will be *cast into hell.*

Hell is fearful. It is described in the Bible as a *place of torment;* a *furnace of fire;* a place of *everlasting burnings* and *unquenchable fire.* It is a place of suffering, with *weeping and* *gnashing of teeth* and in which there is *no rest day or night*. These are terrible words, but they are true. Those in hell are cut off from all good, cursed by God and banished from even the smallest help or comfort that his presence brings.

Hell is final. All roads to hell are one-way streets. There is no exit. Between hell and heaven *there is a great gulf fixed.* The horror, loneliness and agony of hell are not in order to purify but to punish – for ever!

Hell is fair. The Bible tells us that God will *judge the world in righteousness* and he is perfectly just in sending sinners to hell. After all, he is giving them what they have chosen. They reject God here; he rejects them there. They choose to live ungodly lives; he confirms their choice – for ever. God can hardly be accused of injustice or unfairness!

In the light of these terrible truths, you need to think very carefully about a question once put to a group of people in the New Testament: *How can you escape the condemnation of hell?*

Can religion help?

Man has been called a religious animal. *The Encyclopaedia of Religion and Ethics* lists hundreds of ways in which men have tried to satisfy their religious longings and feelings. They have worshipped the sun, moon and stars; earth, fire and water; idols of wood, stone and metal; fish, birds and animals. They have worshipped countless gods and spirits which have been the product of their own perverted imagination. Others have attempted to worship the true God through a vast variety of sacrifices, ceremonies, sacraments and services. But 'religion', however sincere, can never solve man's sin problem, for at least three reasons.

Religion can never satisfy God. Religion is man's attempt to make himself right with God, but any such attempt is futile because even man's best efforts are flawed and so are unacceptable to God. The Bible could not be clearer: *all our righteousnesses are like filthy rags.* God demands perfection; religion fails to meet the demand.

20

Religion can never remove sin. Your virtues can never cancel out your vices. Good deeds can never remove bad ones. If a person gets right with God it is *not of works, lest anyone should boast.* No religious efforts or experiences –christening, confirmation, baptism, holy communion, churchgoing, prayers, gifts, sacrifices of time and effort, Bible reading or anything else – can cancel out a single sin.

Religion can never change man's sinful nature. A person's behaviour is not the problem, only the symptom. The heart of man's problem is the problem of man's heart, and by nature man's heart is corrupt and depraved. Going to church and taking part in religious ceremonies may make you feel good, but they cannot make you good. *Who can bring a clean thing out of an unclean? No one!*

Some of the religious activities mentioned above are obviously 'good' in themselves. For example, it is right to go to church, to read the Bible and to pray, because God tells us to do these things. But you dare not rely on them to make you right with God. Not only are they powerless to do so; trusting in them actually adds to your sin and to your condemnation.

Is there an answer?

Yes there is! – and God has provided it. The central message of the Bible is summed up in these words: *For God so loved the world that he gave his only begotten Son, that whoever believes in him should not perish but have everlasting life.*

We saw earlier that a just and holy God must punish sin. But the Bible also tells us that *God is love.* While God hates sin he loves sinners and longs to forgive them. But how can a sinner be justly pardoned when God's law demands his spiritual and physical death? Only God could solve that problem, and he did so in the person of Jesus Christ. *The Father has sent the Son as Saviour of the world.*

God the Son became man by taking upon himself human nature. Although Jesus became fully man, he remained fully God: the Bible says that *in him dwells all the fullness of the Godhead bodily.* He remained as completely God as if he had not become man; he became as completely man as if he were not God. Jesus Christ is therefore unique and the Bible confirms this in many ways. His conception was unique; he had no human father but was conceived in a virgin's womb by the miraculous power of the Holy Spirit. His words were unique: people were *astonished at his teaching, for his word was with authority.* His miracles were unique: he went about *healing all kinds of sickness and all kinds of disease among the people* and on several occasions even raised the dead. His character was unique: he was *tempted as we are, yet without sin* so that God the Father could say of him, *'This is my beloved Son, in whom I am well pleased.'*

Notice that last sentence! This means that as a man Jesus kept the law of God in every part and therefore was not subject to sin's double death penalty. Yet he was arrested on a trumped-up charge, sentenced on false evidence, and eventually crucified at Jerusalem. But his death was not a 'freak' or unavoidable accident. It was all part of *the carefully planned intention and foreknowledge of God.* The Father sent the Son for the very purpose of paying sin's death penalty, and Jesus willingly came. In his own words, the purpose of his coming into the world was *to give his life a ransom for many.* His death, like his life was unique.

This makes it vital that you understand what happened when Jesus died, and what his death can mean to you.

Why the cross?

All the Bible's teaching points to the death of Jesus. Neither his perfect life nor his marvellous teaching nor his powerful miracles are the focus of the Bible's message. These are all important, but above all else Jesus came into the world to die. What makes his death so important? The answer is that he died as a Substitute, a Sin-bearer and a Saviour.

Jesus the Substitute. This demonstrates the love of God. Sinners are guilty, lost and helpless in the face of God's holy law, which demands punishment for every sin. How can they possibly escape God's righteous wrath? The Bible's answer is this: *God demonstrates his own love towards us, in that while we were still sinners, Christ died for us.* As part of an amazing rescue plan God the Son volunteered to take the place of sinners and bear the just penalty for their sin. The sinless Son of God willingly suffered and died for them, *the just for the unjust.*

Jesus the Sin-bearer. This demonstrates the holiness of God. There was nothing 'faked' about Christ's death. The penalty for the sins of others was paid in full by the death of God's sinless Son.

As he hung on the cross he cried out, *My God, my God, why have you forsaken me?* At that terrible moment God the father turned his back on his beloved Son, who then endured the penalty of separation from God. Notice how this shows God's perfect holiness. All sin, every sin, must be punished – and when Jesus took the place of sinners he became as accountable for their sins as if he had been responsible for them. The one man who lived a perfect life suffered the double death penalty of the guilty.

Jesus the Saviour. This demonstrates the power of God. Three days after his death, Christ was *declared to be the Son of God with power according to the Spirit of holiness, by the resurrection from the dead.* He *presented himself alive after his suffering by many infallible proofs* and Christ *dies no more. Death no longer has dominion over him.* In raising Christ from the dead, God powerfully demonstrated that he accepted his death in the place of sinners as the full and perfect payment of sin's penalty and as the basis on which he can offer a full and free pardon to those who would otherwise be doomed to spend eternity in hell.

But how does all this apply to you? How can you get right with God? How can Christ become your Saviour?

How can I be saved?

Having read this far, do you genuinely want to be saved? Do you want to get right with God – whatever the cost or consequences? If not, you have not grasped the importance of the pages you have read. You should therefore read them again, slowly and carefully, asking God to show you the truth.

If God has shown you your need, and you do want to be saved, then you must have *repentance towards God and faith towards our Lord Jesus Christ.*

You must repent. This means a complete change regarding sin. There must be a change of mind. You must admit that you are a sinner, a rebel against a holy and loving God. There must be a change of heart – genuine sorrow and shame at the vileness and filthiness of your sin. Then you must be willing to forsake it and change the direction of your life. God challenges people to *do works befitting repentance.* You must do this. God will not forgive any sin you are not willing to forsake. To repent is to go in a new direction, seeking wholeheartedly to live in a way that pleases God.

You must have faith in Christ. First of all, this means accepting that Jesus is *Christ, the son of the living God* and that *Christ died for the ungodly.* Secondly, it means believing that in his power and love Christ is able and willing to save you. Thirdly, it means actually putting your trust in Christ, relying upon him and him alone to make you right with God. Your proud, sinful nature will fight against abandoning trust in your own 'goodness' or religion. Yet you have no alternative. You must stop trusting in anything else and trust only in Christ, who is *able to save to the utmost those who come to God through him.*

If God has shown you your need, and given you this desire, then turn to Christ – and do it now! Ideally, pray aloud to him; this may help you to be clear about what you are doing. Confess that you are a guilty, lost and helpless sinner, and with all your heart ask Christ to save you, and to take his rightful place as the Lord of your life, enabling you to turn from sin and to live for him.

The Bible says *that if you confess with your mouth the Lord*

Jesus and believe in your heart that God has raised him from the dead, you will be saved, and that *whoever calls upon the name of the Lord shall be saved.* If you truly trust Christ as your Saviour and acknowledge him as your Lord, you can claim these promises as your own.

Which way now?

If you are trusting in Christ there are many wonderful things in which you can rejoice. For instance, you are now in a right relationship with God: the Bible calls this being 'justified' and says that *having been justified by faith, we have peace with God through our Lord Jesus Christ.* Through Christ, your sins have been dealt with: *through his name, whoever believes in him, will receive remission of sins.* You are now a member of God's family: all who trust in Christ are given *the right to become children of God.* You are eternally secure: *there is therefore now no condemnation to those who are in Christ Jesus.* God himself has come into your life in the person of the Holy Spirit: *the Spirit of him who raised Jesus from the dead dwells in you.* What great truths these are!

Now you need to grow in your new spiritual life. Here are four important things to which you will need to give close attention:

Prayer. You are now able to speak to God as your Father, something you have never been able to do before. You can worship him, praising him for his glory, power, holiness and love. You can ask for daily forgiveness. Not even those who become children of God are perfect, but *if we confess our sins, he is faithful and just to* *forgive us our sins and to cleanse us from all unrighteousness.* You can thank him every day for his goodness to you. There are so many things for which you will want to thank him, including the everyday benefits of life that we can so easily take for granted. But you will specially want to thank him for saving you, for accepting you into his family, and for giving you eternal life. You should never find it difficult to do this! You can also ask for his help, strength and guidance in your own life and in the lives of others. In particular, you will want to pray for other people you know who are away from God as you once were.

Bible reading. In prayer, you speak to God; in the Bible, God speaks to you. It is therefore very important that you read it every day, to find out what *is acceptable to the Lord.* As you do this, ask him to enable you to understand its meaning and to obey its teaching, *that you may grow thereby.* If you need help in beginning to study the Bible, send for your free copy of the booklet mentioned on page 31.

Fellowship. Now that you have become a member of God's family, he wants you to meet regularly with your brothers and sisters; *not forsaking the assembling of ourselves together, …but exhorting one another.* This means joining a local church, so make sure that you do this as soon as possible. Choosing the right church is not always easy, and you will want to find one which clearly believes and teaches the biblical truths you have been reading in these pages. The person who gave you this booklet should be able to help you. In your local church you will find out more about God; you will benefit from the experience of others; you will learn the importance of God's special directions about baptism and holy communion; and you will discover the joy of sharing with others the gifts and abilities God has given you. You need the church, and the church needs you!

Service. It will now be your privilege *to serve the Lord your God with all your heart and with all your soul.* Always remember that God *has saved us and called us with a holy calling.* Make holiness an absolute priority; *for this is the will of God, your sanctification.* Then, seek to use your particular gifts in God's service; bear in mind that you were *created in Christ Jesus for good works.* Finally, be alert for opportunities of telling others *what great things the Lord has done for you.* Telling others about Christ is not only the duty of those who trust him, it is an exhilarating experience!

From now on seek to live in such a way that in every part of your life you *proclaim the praises of him who called you out of darkness into his marvellous light.*

If you have trusted Christ through reading this booklet, and would like help in your daily Bible reading, you are invited to write to John Blanchard, c/o Evangelical Press, Faverdale North, Darlington, DL3 0PH, England, for a free copy of Read, Mark, Learn, his book of guidelines for personal Bible study based on Mark's Gospel.

If you need further help please contact the following person:

125 Schoolhouse Road
Egg Harbor Township, NJ 08234
609-927-3838

Bible references used in this book are as follows:

Page 4
Hebrews 11:6
Genesis 1:1
Hebrews 11:3
Psalm 33:9

Page 5
Acts 17:24
Genesis 2:7
Psalm 139:14

Page 6
Job 11:7
Psalm 19:1
Romans 1:20

Page 7
2 Peter 1:21
Psalm 19:7-8
2 Timothy 3:16
1 Thessalonians 2:13

Page 8
Jeremiah 10:10
Isaiah 44:6
Philippians 2:11
John 1:1
2 Corinthians 3:18

Page 9
John 4:24
John 1:18
Jeremiah 23:24
Psalm 90:2
Revelation 1:8
Malachi 3:6
Acts 17:25

Page 10
Exodus 15:11
1 Samuel 2:2
Habakkuk 1:13
1 Peter 1:16
Isaiah 30:18
Psalm 97:2
Hebrews 4:13
Romans 11:33

Page 11
Psalm 135:6
Ephesians 1:11
Daniel 4:35
Jeremiah 32:27
Job 5:9
Job 37:23

Page 12
Genesis 1:27
Genesis 1:28

Page 13
Genesis 1:31

Page 14
Romans 5:12
Genesis 2:17
Genesis 3:6
Genesis 3:8

Page 15
Romans 5:12
1 John 1:8
Romans 3:23

Page 16
Jeremiah 17:9
Mark 7: 21-22

Page 17
Proverbs 20:9
1 John 3:4
Psalm 7:11
Romans 14:12

Page 18
Hebrews 9:27
2Thessalonians 1:9
Matthew 23:33
Matthew 5:9
Luke 16:28
Matthew 13:42
Isaiah 33:14

Page 19
Matthew 3:12
Matthew 22:13
Revelation 14:11
Luke 16:26
Acts 17:31
Matthew 23:33

Page 20
Isaiah 64:6

Page 21
Ephesians 2:9
Job 14:4

Page 22
John 3:16
1 John 4:8

1 John 4:14
Colossians 2:9

Page 23
Luke 4:32
Matthew 4:23
Hebrews 4:15
Matthew 3:17
Acts 2:23
Matthew 20:28

Page 24
Romans 5:8
1 Peter 3:18

Page 25
Mark 15:34
Romans 1:4
Acts 1:3
Romans 6:9

Page 26
Acts 20:21
Acts 26:20
Matthew 16:16
Romans 5:6

Page 27
Hebrews 7:25
Romans 10:9
Romans 10:13

Page 28
Romans 5:1
Acts 10:43
John 1:12
Romans 8:1
Romans 8:11
1 John 1:9

Page 29
Ephesians 5:10
1 Peter 2:2
Hebrews 10:25

Page 30
Deuteronomy 10:12
2Timothy 1:9
1 Thessalonians 4:3
Ephesians 2:10
Mark 5:19
1 Peter 2:9